AF480677

LIVING YOUR LEGACY, LEADING WITH EXAMPLE

INSPIRING OTHERS THROUGH LIVED VALUES

DR. MINAKSHI BANSAL

DEDICATION

This book is dedicated to all the unsung heroes in leadership—those who lead with quiet strength, unwavering values, and a deep commitment to fostering environments where others can thrive. Your example is a beacon that guides the way forward, illuminating the path for others to follow. May your integrity and dedication inspire generations to come.

♡♡♡

Contents

Contents

Prayer

"Om Bhadram Karnebhih Shrinuyama Devah
Bhadram Pashyemakshabhiryajatrah
Sthirairangais Tushtuvamsastanubhih
Vyashema Devahitam Yadayuh
Svasti Na Indro Vriddhashravah
Svasti Nah Pusha Vishwavedah
Svasti Nastarkshyo Arishtanemih
Svasti No Brihaspatir Dadhatu
Om Shantih Shantih Shantih"

This mantra is a prayer for universal well-being, invoking the blessings of various deities for protection, health, and happiness. It emphasizes the importance of experiencing the auspicious through all senses and living a life aligned with divine purpose. The repetition of "Shantih" at the end signifies a deep desire for peace in the individual, the environment, and the universe at large. This mantra is often recited as a prayer for peace, prosperity, and the physical and spiritual well-being of all beings.

ᐧᐧᐧ

About The Author

Dr. Minakshi Bansal, born in the bustling metropolis of Delhi, India, has led a life steeped in artistry, scholarly pursuit, and an unwavering commitment to societal betterment. Following her marriage, she relocated to Ahmedabad, Gujarat, where she has since blossomed into a multifaceted beacon of inspiration for many. Dr. Minakshi is not only recognized as a gifted artist in the realm of Fine Arts but also as an esteemed author, a devoted social worker and a dedicated research scholar in Psychology. Her journey, marked by a profound dedication to elevating those around her, especially the downtrodden and underprivileged children of society, is a testament to her deep-seated belief in the transformative power of engagement and empathy.

From her earliest days, Minakshi was distinguished by an insatiable appetite for reading. Her literary universe was inhabited by characters and narratives that spanned ethical tales, motivational and inspirational stories, and the mythic parables imbued with life lessons. This voracious reading habit was not merely for personal edification but was driven by a desire to distill and disseminate the essence of these narratives to foster the development of students and peers alike. She was particularly captivated by the lives and teachings of historical figures and spiritual leaders such as Adi Shankaracharya, Swami Vivekananda, Dr. APJ Abdul Kalam, Mahamana Pandit Madan Mohan Malviya, Mahatma Gandhi, Sardar Vallabhai Patel, and Vinoba Bhave, among others. Their philosophies and life stories fueled her ambition to embody their ideals of resilience, selflessness, and relentless pursuit of knowledge.

Dr. Minakshi's academic and practical engagement with psychology has been equally noteworthy. As a research scholar, her focus has been on exploring the intricate tapestry of the human psyche, aiming to unlock the potential for psychological well-being and societal harmony. Her scholarly work is complemented by her active involvement in social work, where she employs her academic insights to make tangible differences in the lives of the underprivileged. Her endeavours in social work are characterized by an innovative approach that combines traditional wisdom with contemporary psychological practices to address the multifaceted challenges faced by these communities.

Her artistic talents, another facet of her diverse capabilities, are not merely a personal passion but also serve as a medium through which she communicates and connects with others. Her art, rich in symbolism and emotional depth, reflects her philosophical inquiries and social concerns, offering viewers a glimpse into the breadth of her intellect and the depth of her compassion.

In addition to her contributions to the arts and social sciences, Dr. Minakshi has embraced the healing arts of Pranic Healing, mastering the techniques developed by Master Choa Kok Sui. This practice, which focuses on the manipulation of Prana or life energy to heal the body and aura, has been both a personal journey of discovery and a means through which she extends her healing touch to others. Her proficiency in Pranic Healing is complemented by her advocacy and teaching of various forms of meditation aimed at rejuvenation, personal betterment, and the cultivation of harmony within individuals and communities alike.

Dr. Minakshi's life is a narrative of relentless pursuit, not just of personal achievement but of the upliftment and empowerment of society at large. Her diverse interests and talents—spanning the arts, literature, psychology, and the healing practices—converge on a singular path of service. She embodies the spirit of the luminaries who inspired her, channelling their legacy through her actions and teachings. Through her books, art, and social initiatives, she continues to inspire a new generation to embark on their own journeys of self-discovery, resilience, and altruism.

Her commitment to social betterment, particularly her focus on uplifting underprivileged children, reflects a deep understanding of the transformative potential of education and personal development. By integrating her knowledge of psychology, her artistic sensibilities, and her healing practices, Dr. Bansal has developed a holistic approach to social work that addresses both the immediate needs and the long-term well-being of the communities she serves.

As an author, Dr. Minakshi's writings offer a blend of inspirational insights, practical wisdom, and reflective contemplations drawn from her extensive reading and life experiences. Her books serve as a guide for those seeking to navigate the complexities of life with grace, resilience, and purpose. Through her narratives, she extends an invitation to her readers to explore the depths of their own potential and to contribute meaningfully to the collective well-being of society.

In Dr. Minakshi Bansal, we find a remarkable synthesis of the artist, the scholar, the healer, and the social activist. Her life's work stands as a beacon of hope and a source of inspiration for individuals seeking to make a difference in the world. Her story is a compelling reminder of the power of individual action, rooted in compassion and driven by a profound commitment to the betterment of humanity. Dr. Minakshi's legacy is not just in the tangible outcomes of her efforts but in the enduring spirit of inquiry, empathy, and service that she embodies.

ᑭᑭᑭ

Preface

In the world of leadership, where actions reverberate more loudly than words, the essence of one's legacy is often captured not in the milestones achieved but in the values lived. It is these values that shape our interactions, influence our decisions, and ultimately define our contributions to the world. This book is born out of the belief that leadership is not just a role to be executed but a life to be lived purposefully, with each decision and action reflecting a deep commitment to personal and professional values.

The journey of writing this book has been a profound exploration of what it means to lead with integrity, empathy, and foresight. It delves into the myriad ways in which a leader can inspire, influence, and leave an indelible mark on both their immediate surroundings and the broader world. At its core, the book champions the concept that true leadership transcends the confines of boardrooms and strategic meetings, reaching into the community and across generations.

Throughout this exploration, I have drawn upon a multitude of sources, from established theories and models of leadership to the less tangible but equally important lessons gleaned from everyday experiences. The insights shared here are complemented by stories of real-life leaders who have exemplified living their values in both ordinary and extraordinary ways. These narratives not only serve as a testament to the power of values-driven leadership but also provide practical examples that readers can aspire to and emulate.

The significance of living one's values cannot be overstressed in today's ever-evolving global landscape, where leaders are constantly tested by shifting economic tides, cultural transformations, and technological advancements. In such a context, the steadfastness of a leader's values acts as a compass, guiding their actions and decisions through the complexities of modern governance and management. This book, therefore, is not just about the theoretical underpinnings of leadership but also about the practical application of values in day-to-day leadership scenarios.

One of the fundamental themes of this work is the concept of reflection and projection—looking inward to understand one's values and outward to anticipate how these values can impact the world. This dual approach ensures that leadership is both introspective and outward-looking, balancing self-awareness with a sense of responsibility towards others. Each chapter of the book builds on this theme, presenting ideas and strategies that help leaders understand and implement their values in various aspects of their life and work.

Moreover, the narrative underscores the importance of resilience and adaptability, qualities that are indispensable for any leader aiming to leave a lasting legacy. In a world where change is the only constant, the ability to adapt one's leadership style and strategies to meet evolving circumstances is as crucial as having a firm grasp of one's core values.

The role of technology in amplifying a leader's values and legacy also receives significant attention. In an age where digital platforms can extend one's influence far beyond traditional physical boundaries, understanding how to effectively use these tools is crucial for any leader wishing to make a broader impact.

This book also addresses the critical aspect of health and well-being in leadership. The physical and mental demands of leadership are immense, and maintaining one's health is essential for sustained effectiveness. The discussion extends beyond personal health to consider how leaders can foster environments that promote overall well-being and productivity.

Lastly, the exploration of mentoring and coaching highlights the importance of nurturing the next generation of leaders. The legacy of a leader is not only in the achievements accrued during their tenure but also in the wisdom they impart to those who will follow. The chapters devoted to these aspects provide a guide on how leaders can effectively mentor and coach others, ensuring that their values live on through the successes of their protégés.

In writing this book, my aim has been to inspire leaders at all levels to reflect deeply on the legacy they wish to leave. It is my hope that the insights and strategies discussed will not only enrich the reader's understanding of leadership but also empower them to lead in ways that make a meaningful and lasting difference. As we navigate the complexities of our roles, may we all strive to lead by example, inspired by the firm belief that how we lead is as important as what we achieve.

ONE

DEFINING YOUR LEGACY

Understanding what constitutes a legacy is crucial for anyone aspiring to lead and inspire others. A legacy isn't merely about the material possessions or the accolades one leaves behind; it encompasses the imprint one leaves on the world through their actions, decisions, and the values they champion. This broader definition shifts the focus from tangible achievements to the more profound impacts of personal values and ethics.

Personal values are at the core of defining one's legacy. These values act as a compass that guides behavior, influences decisions, and shapes interactions with others. Whether it's integrity, compassion, or courage, these values are reflected in every action a leader takes. When consistently applied, they become synonymous with the individual's name, defining how they are remembered and the legacy they leave.

One of the first steps in defining your legacy is self-reflection. This involves taking the time to consider what values are most important to you. What principles do you hold dear? What do you want to be known for? This reflective process is not a one-time activity but a continuous one, where a leader consistently evaluates their actions and decisions to ensure they align with their chosen values.

After identifying these core values, the next step is to integrate them into your daily life. This is where the concept of 'living your values' comes into play. It's not enough to simply state what you believe in; you must also act on these beliefs. For example, if you value honesty, then honesty must be evident in all your communications and dealings, both within and outside your professional life. Living your values is what builds trust and credibility with others, which is essential for any leader.

Another crucial aspect of defining your legacy is considering the impact of your actions on others. Leadership is inherently relational, and the way you interact with people can significantly influence your legacy. Are you uplifting and empowering those around you? Do your actions encourage others to embrace and act on their values? Inspiring others to reflect and act on their values can amplify the reach of your legacy, creating a ripple effect that extends far beyond your immediate circle.

It's also important to recognize that defining a legacy is not just about the end of a career or life. It's about living each day with the end in mind. This perspective helps in making more purposeful choices and in considering the long-term effects of today's actions. Every decision, no matter how small, contributes to the legacy you are building.

Finally, communicating your values and legacy aspirations can help others understand and support your vision. Sharing your journey and the reasons behind your actions can inspire others to consider their own legacies. It can foster a culture of introspection and purpose-driven action, which is essential for any community or organization looking to make a lasting impact.

Defining your legacy is a dynamic and intentional process. It requires deep self-awareness, consistent alignment of actions with personal values, and a commitment to impact others positively. By choosing to live a life that reflects your deepest values, you not only enrich your own life but also inspire others to think about the legacy they wish to create. Your legacy becomes a beacon that can guide future generations, extending your influence far beyond your immediate presence.

❧❧❧

"True leadership is measured not by the heights one reaches, but by the depth of their commitment to values that elevate everyone around them."

❧❧❧

TWO

THE POWER OF EXAMPLE

Leadership transcends the confines of titles and positions, asserting its influence most profoundly through the power of example. This silent force of personal example sets the tone for behavior and establishes standards of excellence that can inspire entire organizations or communities. The impact of role models in shaping not just careers but also personal lives is profound and far-reaching, illustrating the essential nature of leading by example.

Role models serve as tangible proof that certain qualities, behaviors, and actions lead to success and fulfillment. They provide a roadmap for others to follow, demonstrating the potential outcomes of perseverance, ethical behavior, and dedication. When leaders embody the qualities they wish to instill in their followers, they create a compelling narrative that encourages others to emulate these traits. The authenticity of leading by example also cultivates trust and respect, which are crucial components of effective leadership.

The influence of a good role model can be seen in every sphere of life, from education and sports to business and politics. For instance, a teacher who exhibits a passion for learning can ignite a lifelong love of education in students. Similarly, a manager who practices open communication and fairness can foster a workplace culture that values transparency and equity, encouraging employees to express their ideas and concerns without fear of reprisal.

Leading by example is particularly effective in instilling values and ethical behavior. When leaders demonstrate integrity and accountability in their actions, they send a clear message that these values are non-negotiable within the organization. This approach not only helps in establishing a moral compass but also deters unethical behavior by setting a high standard for everyone to follow. Additionally, when leaders face ethical dilemmas or challenges, their methods of dealing with these situations teach more about real-world ethics than any seminar or training program could.

The concept of "do as I do, not just as I say" should be a guiding principle for anyone in a leadership role. This not only involves showing excellence in day-to-day tasks but also showing how to handle mistakes and failures. Leaders who are open about their challenges and how they overcome them provide valuable lessons in resilience and determination. Such transparency also humanizes leaders, making them more relatable and approachable to their followers.

Moreover, leading by example involves the demonstration of soft skills that are crucial in today's collaborative work environments. Skills such as empathy, patience, and the ability to listen are often more effectively taught through actions rather than words. A leader who listens actively to others and shows empathy can create a supportive environment where everyone feels valued and understood. This kind of environment is conducive to innovation and creativity as team members feel secure in expressing their ideas and taking risks.

The ripple effect of leading by example is also significant. Individuals who observe positive and effective leadership behaviors in their role models are likely to adopt these behaviors themselves, which in turn influences others in their personal and professional circles. This chain reaction can amplify the impact of a single good leader exponentially.

However, the power of example is not limited to positive influences. Negative examples can have an equally powerful, albeit destructive, impact. Leaders who exhibit unethical behavior, lack of commitment, or disinterest in their roles can demoralize their teams, erode trust, and encourage similar behaviors in others. Therefore, the responsibility of being a role model is a significant aspect of leadership that should be wielded with care and consideration.

The power of example is a fundamental aspect of leadership that extends beyond mere professional guidance. It is about inspiring others through one's own actions, which speaks louder than any words could. This approach not only builds better leaders but also fosters communities and organizations that reflect the core values and ethics exemplified by their leaders. True leadership is about showing the way, not just telling the way, making the power of example a pivotal element in the legacy any leader hopes to leave behind.

ppp

"A leader's real influence is felt in the quiet moments of decision, where their values become the compass that steers their actions."

ᐅᐅᐅ

THREE
CRAFTING YOUR VISION

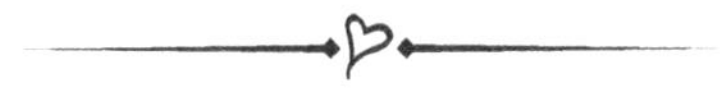

The foundation of any successful endeavor, be it personal or professional, lies in a clear and compelling vision. Crafting a vision involves envisioning a future that motivates and guides you, providing a roadmap for the decisions and actions you undertake. A well-defined vision acts as a beacon, helping to navigate through challenges and keeping focus aligned with long-term goals. This essential leadership task not only defines what you aspire to achieve but also impacts those around you, setting a precedent for what can be accomplished.

Developing a clear vision begins with introspection and understanding what truly matters to you. It requires you to dig deep into your values, interests, and desires to determine what drives you. What are your passions? What change do you wish to see in your world or your community? How do you want to influence those around you? Answering these questions can provide the initial direction needed to formulate your vision.

Once you have a sense of what drives you, the next step is to articulate these ideas into a coherent vision statement. This statement should be concise yet inspiring, specific enough to provide guidance but broad enough to allow for growth and evolution. It should encapsulate your highest priorities and reflect your core values. A vision statement is not just a declaration of future goals; it is a reflection of the impact you envision.

Translating personal values and ambitions into a professional vision involves aligning your career objectives with your personal values. This alignment ensures that your professional actions and decisions not only advance your career but also contribute to your broader life goals. For example, if one of your core values is innovation, your professional vision might focus on creating environments where new ideas are fostered and valued.

Implementing your vision requires setting specific, measurable, achievable, relevant, and time-bound (SMART) goals. These goals act as stepping stones towards achieving your vision. By breaking down your vision into actionable objectives, you make it manageable and trackable. This step-by-step approach ensures that each action you take contributes towards the larger picture you have envisioned.

Communication plays a vital role in making your vision impactful. Sharing your vision with others not only helps to garner support and commitment but also invites feedback and collaboration. Whether in a professional setting or a personal context, articulating your vision clearly can inspire others and potentially attract like-minded individuals or allies who can aid in achieving your goals. Effective communication of your vision can transform it from a personal guide into a collective endeavor.

Moreover, a vision must be dynamic. It should evolve as you gain more experiences and insights. Regularly revisiting and potentially revising your vision statement ensures that it remains relevant and resonant with your current beliefs and circumstances. Life's unpredictability might lead you to new interests or away from old ones, and your vision must reflect these shifts to stay meaningful and motivating.

In addition to crafting and implementing a vision, it is crucial to embody it. You must live in a manner that consistently reflects your vision. This embodiment not only reinforces your commitment to your goals but also strengthens your credibility and leadership. When others see you actively pursuing your vision, it can motivate them to engage in their pursuits or support yours.

In conclusion, crafting a vision is a powerful process that shapes not only your future actions but also influences those around you. It is a dynamic and continuous journey that involves deep self-exploration, clear articulation, and steadfast commitment to your values and goals. Through careful planning, effective communication, and consistent action, your vision can lead you to not just meet but exceed your personal and professional aspirations, serving as a guiding light in your leadership journey and beyond.

ᗁᗁᗁ

"Leading by example isn't just about what we do when everyone is watching; it's about the choices we make when no one may ever know."

▷▷▷

FOUR
VALUES IN ACTION

Incorporating core values into daily actions is essential for personal integrity and professional success. Values guide decisions, influence behavior, and shape interactions with others. They serve as a compass that directs your life and work, ensuring that your actions consistently reflect your deepest beliefs and aspirations. Putting values into practice is not just about adhering to ethical standards; it's about making your values visible and active in every aspect of your life.

The first step in putting values into action is to clearly define what those values are. This requires thoughtful introspection and honest self-assessment. What principles are non-negotiable in your life? Common examples include honesty, respect, responsibility, fairness, and compassion. These values should be explicitly identified and articulated so they can serve as a foundation for behavior and decision-making.

Once your values are defined, the next challenge is to operationalize them—turning abstract concepts into concrete actions. This involves setting specific behaviors that reflect each value. For instance, if one of your core values is transparency, operationalizing this value might mean openly sharing your decision-making processes and being clear about your intentions in both personal and professional contexts. Similarly, if you value compassion, you might prioritize empathy and listening skills, ensuring that you are attentive to the emotions and needs of others.

Integrating values into daily life also requires mindfulness. It's one thing to know your values and another to be mindful of them in the rush of daily activities. Mindfulness in this context means maintaining an acute awareness of how your values should guide your actions in real-time. This could be as simple as taking a brief moment to reflect on your values before making decisions or interacting with others.

Values are also put into practice through consistent habits. Forming habits that align with your values can help make value-driven behavior more automatic over time. For example, if you value lifelong learning, you might develop the habit of reading for an hour each day or dedicating time each week to attend workshops or lectures. These habits reinforce your values and integrate them into the regular rhythm of your life.

Another critical aspect of putting values into action is accountability. Holding yourself accountable involves regularly checking if your actions align with your values. This can be achieved through self-reflection, seeking feedback from others, and setting up systems to monitor your behavior. Accountability partners, whether mentors, colleagues, or friends, can also play a vital role. They can provide external perspectives and remind you of your commitments when you stray from them.

Values in action also manifest through leadership and influence. Leaders who actively demonstrate their values not only reinforce these principles in their own lives but also inspire others to adopt similar behaviors. This form of leadership by example can profoundly impact an organization or community, cultivating a culture where core values are shared and enacted by all members.

Moreover, living your values openly and consistently can sometimes lead to conflict, particularly when they clash with those of others or with prevailing practices in a workplace or community. Navigating these conflicts requires courage and negotiation skills, standing firm on your values while respecting differing viewpoints. It also involves finding common ground where possible and influencing change through persuasion and example.

Putting values into action is not a passive endeavor. It requires deliberate intention, constant attention, and active implementation. By defining clear values, setting specific behaviors to embody those values, practicing mindfulness, forming supporting habits, maintaining accountability, and demonstrating leadership, you can ensure that your core values are not just abstract ideals but living, breathing parts of your everyday life. This continuous commitment to living your values not only enhances your own sense of integrity and satisfaction but also sets a powerful example for others to follow.

ᐅᐅᐅ

"Resilience in leadership means standing strong in the face of adversity, turning challenges into stepping stones for growth and learning."

▷▷▷

FIVE

THE ROLE OF INTEGRITY

Integrity is often cited as one of the most valued traits in individuals, particularly in leaders. It is not just about being honest but about being consistent between what one says and what one does. This consistency is crucial for building trust, credibility, and respect, both in personal relationships and in professional environments. The importance of integrity lies in its ability to foster environments of openness and fairness, which are essential for effective collaboration and sustainable success.

The essence of integrity begins with alignment—ensuring that your words match your actions. This alignment is not always straightforward, as it requires a deep understanding of one's values and the courage to live by them, even when faced with challenges or when it would be easier to compromise. The real test of integrity comes at times of temptation or pressure; it is in these moments that integrity is both most difficult to uphold and most crucial.

One of the primary reasons integrity is so important is that it builds trust. Trust is the foundation of all relationships, whether with colleagues, friends, family, or customers. When people see that you are consistent in your words and actions, they are more likely to believe that you will follow through on your promises in the future. This trust facilitates smoother interactions, quicker decision-making, and increased willingness to share information and resources.

In professional settings, the integrity of leaders is especially significant. Leaders set the tone for the organization's culture and ethical standards. When leaders demonstrate integrity, they create an ethical framework for the entire organization to follow. This can lead to a more positive workplace environment, enhanced job satisfaction, and improved loyalty among employees. Conversely, a lack of integrity in leadership can lead to a toxic work culture, where shortcuts, dishonesty, and mistrust are prevalent.

Integrity also plays a vital role in accountability. When leaders and individuals consistently act with integrity, they hold themselves and others to a high standard of fairness and ethical behavior. This accountability ensures that everyone is treated equally and that actions are judged based on consistent standards. Accountability, supported by integrity, helps in maintaining organizational justice and can prevent unethical behaviors such as corruption, bias, and nepotism.

Furthermore, integrity is essential for effective communication. When you are known for your integrity, your words carry more weight. People are more likely to listen to and consider your viewpoints if they trust that you are sincere and that your actions align with your statements. This trust can enhance your influence and leadership, as others are more likely to follow your lead and take your advice.

However, maintaining integrity is not without challenges. It often requires making tough decisions, sometimes at the expense of personal gain or popularity. For example, it might mean admitting a mistake when you could have easily covered it up, or standing up for what is right when it is unpopular. These decisions can be difficult, but they are necessary for maintaining one's integrity.

To cultivate and maintain integrity, it is helpful to:

Regularly reflect on your values and ensure your decisions align with these values.

Set clear ethical guidelines for yourself and your organization.

Communicate openly and honestly, especially when facing difficult situations.

Hold yourself and others accountable when there are discrepancies between words and actions.

Integrity is not just a moral choice but a practical strategy for building trust, credibility, and respect. Its importance transcends personal benefit and affects the broader community and organizational health. By prioritizing consistency between words and actions, individuals can lead more effectively, foster more productive relationships, and create a legacy of trust and respect that lasts beyond their tenure. The commitment to integrity is a commitment to a life of coherence where actions and words are in harmony, creating a reliable and admirable personal and professional identity.

ppp

"The legacy of a great leader is woven through the lives they touch, the culture they nurture, and the values they live and leave behind."

ᐅᐅᐅ

SIX

EMPATHY AS A LEADERSHIP TOOL

Empathy, the ability to understand and share the feelings of another, is increasingly recognized as a critical component in effective leadership. Far from being a soft or unnecessary skill, empathy can enhance leadership effectiveness, improve workplace relationships, and drive organizational success. Empathetic leadership fosters an environment of trust and respect, which are essential for collaboration and innovation.

Empathy in leadership means genuinely understanding the emotions, thoughts, and experiences of others without judgment. This understanding helps leaders make more informed decisions that consider the impacts on all stakeholders involved. It also contributes to a more inclusive work environment where diverse perspectives are valued and integrated into the decision-making process.

One of the primary benefits of empathetic leadership is improved communication. When leaders are empathetic, they are better equipped to understand the underlying messages and emotions in communications with team members. This can lead to clearer and more effective exchanges, as leaders can address concerns and motivations that might not be explicitly stated. Furthermore, when employees feel understood, they are more likely to express their ideas and concerns, leading to a more open and communicative workplace.

Empathy also enhances team collaboration. Understanding and appreciating the diverse emotional and intellectual contributions of team members can help in crafting strategies that leverage these strengths, leading to more effective teamwork. Teams guided by empathetic leaders often exhibit higher levels of engagement and cooperation because each member feels valued and understood, which motivates them to contribute more actively to the team's objectives.

Moreover, empathy contributes to conflict resolution. Conflicts in the workplace are inevitable, but how they are handled can make a significant difference in organizational health. Empathetic leaders can navigate conflicts more effectively because they can see and understand different perspectives, allowing them to mediate discussions and find solutions that are acceptable to all parties involved.

By addressing the emotional and relational aspects of conflict, empathetic leaders help maintain a positive work environment even in times of disagreement.

Leadership empathy also plays a crucial role in driving change. Change management involves guiding people through uncertainty and new challenges, a process during which empathy is invaluable. Leaders who demonstrate empathy can better gauge their team's reactions to change and provide the support needed to facilitate smooth transitions.

Additionally, by understanding the concerns and resistances of their teams, leaders can tailor their communication and change strategies to mitigate fears and encourage acceptance.

Empathy in leadership also affects employee development. An empathetic leader can recognize the unique needs, aspirations, and potential of each employee. This awareness allows leaders to tailor development opportunities that not only align with the organization's goals but also with the personal and professional growth goals of individual team members.

This personalized approach to development can lead to more effective and fulfilling growth paths for employees, which in turn can enhance loyalty and retention.

Furthermore, demonstrating empathy contributes to a leader's ability to inspire and motivate. Leaders who show genuine concern for the well-being and success of their employees can inspire a high level of commitment and effort. Employees are more likely to go above and beyond for leaders they feel truly care about them as individuals, not just as workers.

However, developing and exhibiting empathy requires practice and intentionality. It involves active listening, where leaders give their full attention to others, reflecting on what is being said and expressing understanding. Leaders can also develop empathy by exposing themselves to diverse perspectives and experiences, which can broaden their understanding of different life experiences and viewpoints.

Empathy is a powerful tool in leadership that enhances interpersonal relationships, team dynamics, conflict resolution, and overall organizational effectiveness. By fostering an empathetic culture, leaders can build more resilient, innovative, and committed teams. The empathetic approach in leadership goes beyond mere sympathy; it involves a strategic and sincere effort to understand, respect, and integrate the diverse emotional landscapes of all team members into a cohesive and supportive work environment.

This not only benefits individuals but also enhances the collective capacity of the organization to navigate challenges and embrace opportunities.

ϷϷϷ

"Effective communication is the bridge between confusion and clarity, a tool that every true leader must master and employ."

ᐅᐅᐅ

SEVEN

RESILIENCE IN LEADERSHIP

Resilience, the capacity to recover quickly from difficulties and adapt to change, is an indispensable quality for leaders. The ever-evolving landscape of the modern workplace, characterized by constant changes, unforeseen challenges, and high demands, necessitates leaders who are not only capable of enduring adversity but also thriving amidst it. Developing resilience can greatly enhance a leader's effectiveness, enabling them to maintain their composure, inspire confidence in their teams, and steer their organizations through turbulent times.

Resiliencc in leadership begins with a mindset that views challenges as opportunities for growth rather than insurmountable obstacles. This mindset, often referred to as a 'growth mindset,' enables leaders to approach difficulties with curiosity and openness, learning from each experience and using it to become stronger. Cultivating this mindset involves recognizing that setbacks are part of the leadership journey and that each setback provides valuable lessons that contribute to personal and professional development.

One effective strategy for building resilience is fostering emotional intelligence (EI). Emotional intelligence, the ability to understand

and manage one's own emotions as well as recognize and influence the emotions of others, is crucial for resilient leadership. Leaders with high EI are better equipped to handle stress, navigate complex interpersonal dynamics, and make balanced decisions under pressure. Developing EI can be facilitated through self-awareness exercises, such as reflective journaling or mindfulness practices, which help leaders become more conscious of their emotional responses and triggers.

Maintaining physical and mental health is also critical for resilience. Stress and challenges can take a toll on a leader's body and mind, making it essential to prioritize health and well-being. This can include regular physical activity, which not only keeps the body healthy but also has proven benefits for mental health, such as reducing anxiety and improving mood. Additionally, ensuring adequate rest and nutrition can help maintain energy levels and cognitive function, which are essential for dealing with high-pressure situations.

Another key element in building resilience is the development of a strong support network. Leaders should cultivate relationships with mentors, peers, and team members who can offer support, guidance, and a fresh perspective during tough times. Having a trusted group of advisers to discuss problems with can provide emotional relief as well as practical solutions that might not have been considered. Support networks can also reinforce a leader's sense of purpose and belonging, which are important for sustaining motivation during challenging periods.

Effective time management and prioritization are further crucial skills for resilient leaders. By managing time efficiently and focusing on what is most important, leaders can reduce overwhelm and prevent burnout. This might involve delegating tasks, setting clear boundaries between work and personal life, and ensuring there are periods built into the schedule for rest and recovery.

Learning to say 'no' to tasks or projects that do not align with key goals or that overextend capacity is also part of effective prioritization.

Additionally, resilient leaders are adept at adaptive thinking, which involves the ability to think creatively about solutions and consider various alternatives when faced with obstacles. This flexibility in thinking helps leaders to not become fixated on one solution or pathway, which might not always be available or effective. Adaptive thinking can be enhanced through practices such as scenario planning, where leaders consider different potential outcomes and develop strategies for each, thereby preparing themselves to shift course quickly if necessary.

Resilient leaders also recognize the importance of celebrating successes and acknowledging the hard work of their teams, even in small victories. This practice can maintain morale and motivation, both for the leader and their team, particularly through long or difficult projects. Recognizing achievements reinforces the value of effort and persistence and can help build collective resilience within a team.

Resilience is not a static quality but a dynamic skill set that leaders can develop and strengthen over time. By adopting a growth mindset, enhancing emotional intelligence, maintaining physical and mental health, developing a supportive network, managing time effectively, practicing adaptive thinking, and celebrating successes, leaders can build their resilience. These strategies not only help leaders handle the challenges they currently face but also equip them with the tools to manage future adversities, leading to sustained effectiveness and success in their roles.

ppp

"*Empathy in leadership is the crucial thread that connects personal struggles to collective triumphs, transforming workplaces into communities.*"

⊳⊳⊳

EIGHT

MINDFUL LEADERSHIP

Mindful leadership embodies the practice of mindfulness—an intentional focus on the present moment, often with a non-judgmental awareness—applied within the context of leading others. This approach not only enhances leaders' decision-making capabilities and stress management skills but also improves their overall effectiveness in guiding their teams. By incorporating mindfulness practices into their daily routines, leaders can develop a clearer, more composed mindset, which is crucial in today's fast-paced and often high-stress work environments.

One of the foundational aspects of mindful leadership is the cultivation of self-awareness. This involves leaders becoming more attuned to their thoughts, feelings, and behaviors. Self-awareness allows leaders to recognize their strengths and weaknesses, understand their emotional triggers, and better manage their responses to stressful situations.

Practices such as daily meditation or quiet reflection can significantly enhance self-awareness. Even a few minutes of focused breathing or mindful walking each day can help leaders center themselves and gain clarity on their mental and emotional states.

Mindful leaders also benefit from the practice of active listening, which is listening with full attention and presence, without prematurely formulating responses or judgments. This form of listening enhances communication within teams and enables leaders to better understand the needs, concerns, and ideas of their colleagues.

Active listening fosters a more inclusive and supportive environment, encouraging open dialogue and collaboration. This can be practiced in every interaction by focusing entirely on the speaker, noting their body language and tone, and reflecting on what is being said before responding.

Another key practice in mindful leadership is the development of emotional regulation. Mindfulness helps leaders manage their emotions more effectively by allowing them to recognize their feelings without being overwhelmed by them.

Techniques such as mindful breathing or pausing before reacting can provide the space needed to choose how to respond to challenging situations thoughtfully rather than impulsively. This ability to regulate emotions is particularly valuable in high-pressure or emotionally charged situations, helping to maintain a calm and productive work environment.

Mindfulness also enhances decision-making. It does so by reducing the noise of constant mental chatter and the influence of past biases or future anxieties. This clearer mental state enables leaders to make more informed, rational decisions based on the current facts and a deeper understanding of their own intuitive judgments.

Leaders can cultivate this aspect of mindfulness through practices like mindfulness meditation, where the focus is on observing thoughts as they arise without attachment, helping to develop a more balanced and centered approach to problem-solving.

Furthermore, stress management is another critical area where mindful leadership proves highly beneficial. Regular mindfulness practice has been shown to lower stress levels by enhancing physiological responses to stress, such as reducing the production of stress hormones like cortisol. Techniques such as guided imagery, progressive muscle relaxation, or simply taking mindful breaks throughout the day can help leaders manage their stress levels effectively.

These practices not only benefit the individual leader but also set a calm and assured tone for the entire team, which can reduce overall workplace stress.

A practice closely related to mindfulness in the context of leadership is gratitude. Maintaining a habit of recognizing and appreciating the positive aspects of one's life and work can shift the focus away from stress and challenges and towards a more positive outlook. This shift can profoundly affect a leader's mood and outlook, influencing their interactions and the morale of their team. Leaders can practice gratitude by starting meetings with acknowledgments of team members' efforts or keeping a personal journal where they note things they are grateful for each day.

Moreover, a mindful leader recognizes the importance of compassion, both towards themselves and others. Compassion involves understanding the difficulties others are facing and taking steps to alleviate them. For leaders, this might mean providing additional support to an overwhelmed team member or fostering a more supportive and understanding workplace culture.

Practicing self-compassion is also vital, as leaders often place high expectations on themselves. Mindful self-compassion can be nurtured through practices like self-kindness and recognition of one's limits and needs.

Mindful leadership is an approach that emphasizes presence, awareness, and compassion. By integrating mindfulness practices into their daily lives, leaders can enhance their decision-making abilities, manage stress more effectively, and create a supportive, productive work environment.

These practices not only benefit the leaders themselves but also positively impact their teams and organizations, promoting a culture of focused calm and deliberate action.

ɷɷɷ

"A crisis doesn't just test a leader's mettle; it reveals
the core of their character, shaping their legacy
through each decision and action."

❧❧❧

NINE

INCLUSIVE LEADERSHIP

Inclusive leadership is a critical approach in today's globalized world, where workplaces are increasingly diverse in terms of ethnicity, gender, age, national origin, disability, sexual orientation, education, and religion. Inclusive leaders actively work to ensure that every individual feels valued and has an equal opportunity to contribute and succeed. This leadership style not only fosters fairness and respect but also drives innovation and enhances organizational performance by leveraging a wide range of perspectives.

The importance of inclusivity and diversity in leadership can be seen first in the broadening of organizational perspective. Diverse teams bring a variety of viewpoints and experiences to the table, which can lead to more creative and innovative solutions. Inclusive leaders harness these diverse perspectives by creating an environment where everyone feels safe and encouraged to express their opinions and ideas. This open exchange can prevent groupthink and introduce new ideas that propel the organization forward.

Inclusive leadership also plays a vital role in attracting and retaining talent. Today's workforce looks for environments where they can feel included and respected. Organizations led by inclusive leaders are more likely to attract a diverse pool of candidates, which not only improves the quality of the workforce but also enhances the company's reputation. Additionally, when employees feel their voices are heard and valued, they are more likely to be satisfied with their jobs and stay with the company, reducing turnover and the associated costs of recruitment and training.

Another key benefit of inclusive leadership is improved decision-making. Inclusive leaders who encourage participation from all team members make decisions that consider multiple perspectives, which are typically more well-rounded and robust against potential problems. This inclusivity in decision-making processes can lead to better outcomes and avoid pitfalls that might occur when decisions are made in a more homogeneous or closed environment.

Inclusive leadership also enhances employee engagement and productivity. Employees who feel included are more likely to be engaged with their work and committed to the organization's goals. This engagement translates into higher productivity and better overall performance. Furthermore, when leaders treat team members equitably and support their development, employees are more likely to go above and beyond in their roles, contributing to organizational success.

Moreover, inclusive leadership is essential for fostering a positive workplace culture. When leaders model inclusivity, it sets a tone that permeates the entire organization. This can create a more supportive and harmonious workplace, where discrimination and biases are actively challenged and addressed. A positive culture not only improves employee morale but also enhances collaboration among team members from different backgrounds.

To effectively practice inclusive leadership, leaders must develop a deep understanding of cultural, societal, and personal differences and how these can influence interactions and perceptions within the workplace. This often involves ongoing education and self-reflection to uncover and mitigate personal biases that can undermine inclusivity efforts.

Inclusive leaders also need to be adept at communication, ensuring that their messaging is accessible and considerate of diverse audiences. This might involve adapting communication styles to fit the needs of different team members or making sure that all team members have access to the same information.

In addition, inclusive leaders must actively promote equity, ensuring that everyone has access to the same opportunities. This might involve implementing mentorship programs, modifying recruitment strategies to reach a broader audience, or offering targeted development programs to ensure all employees can achieve their potential.

Inclusive leadership is not just a moral imperative but a strategic one. It enhances the organization's ability to innovate, improves decision-making, attracts and retains top talent, boosts productivity, and fosters a positive work environment. By committing to an inclusive leadership style, leaders can ensure that all team members feel valued and empowered to contribute their best work, which is essential for the success and sustainability of any organization.

ᗒᗒᗒ

"Technology in leadership is not about showcasing prowess but about expanding reach and influence, turning intentions into impactful actions."

⊳⊳⊳

TEN

MENTORING AND COACHING

Mentoring and coaching are two pivotal strategies in leadership aimed at developing the skills, knowledge, and abilities of others. While they share common goals, the methods and relationships involved can differ significantly. Both play crucial roles in fostering talent within organizations, enhancing professional growth, and ultimately contributing to the success of individuals and teams.

The Role of Mentoring

Mentoring involves a more experienced or knowledgeable person guiding a less experienced or knowledgeable person, often referred to as a mentee. This relationship is typically long-term and focuses on the overall development of the mentee, not just specific skills or objectives. A mentor provides guidance, encouragement, and support to help the mentee navigate their career, improve their skills, and make more informed decisions about their professional development.

Mentors serve as role models and advisors to their mentees, sharing their experiences and insights, which help mentees avoid common pitfalls and accelerate their learning process. The relationship is often personal, with mentors taking a genuine interest in the holistic growth of their mentees. This includes discussions about career opportunities, work-life balance, and personal values, making mentoring a comprehensive approach to professional growth.

One key aspect of effective mentoring is the establishment of trust and confidentiality. This secure environment allows mentees to open up about their fears, challenges, and aspirations, which is crucial for their development. Mentors then use their experience to provide advice and direction tailored to the mentee's individual circumstances, promoting a personalized growth path.

The Role of Coaching

In contrast, coaching tends to be more focused and structured than mentoring, with specific goals and outcomes in mind. Coaches work with individuals (or teams) to improve their performance or enhance their professional skills within a relatively short time frame. Unlike mentors, coaches do not necessarily need to be experts in the field of the individuals they coach but should be skilled in coaching methodologies.

Coaching is highly interactive, relying on asking questions that prompt individuals to reflect deeply about their behaviors, challenges, and goals. This process helps individuals gain clarity about their objectives, uncover hidden barriers to their success, and identify actionable steps to overcome these barriers. Coaches provide support and accountability, helping individuals to stay focused and motivated as they work toward their goals.

The coaching relationship is characterized by its focus on achieving immediate improvements and specific developmental objectives. This could involve enhancing communication skills, leadership abilities, or managing work stress effectively. Coaches use various tools and techniques, such as role-playing, simulations, and feedback models, to develop these skills.

Synergistic Benefits

Both mentoring and coaching are essential for fostering a culture of continuous improvement and learning within organizations. They encourage knowledge sharing, skill development, and professional growth, which are crucial for organizational adaptability and competitiveness.

Additionally, both strategies can significantly impact job satisfaction and retention rates. Employees who are mentored or coached often feel more valued by their organizations, leading to higher levels of engagement and loyalty. This personal investment in employees' growth can also enhance their productivity and efficiency, contributing positively to the organization's bottom line.

Mentoring and coaching also play a critical role in succession planning. By preparing promising employees for future leadership roles through targeted coaching and broad developmental mentoring, organizations can ensure a pipeline of capable leaders. This preparation helps organizations maintain stability and direction even as changes occur within leadership roles.

Implementing Effective Practices

To implement effective mentoring and coaching within an organization, it is important to clearly define the objectives and expectations of these initiatives. For mentoring, pairing the right mentor with the right mentee is crucial, as the personal connection and mutual respect greatly influence the effectiveness of the mentorship.

For coaching, it is essential to train coaches or hire skilled coaches who can apply the most effective techniques to meet the specific developmental needs of their clients. Regular evaluations should also be conducted to assess the effectiveness of the coaching and ensure that the goals are being met.

Mentoring and coaching are invaluable tools in leadership that enhance not only the capabilities and performance of individuals but also contribute to the overall health and success of organizations. By investing in these practices, leaders can develop more skilled, motivated, and engaged teams, ready to meet the challenges of the modern business environment.

ϷϷϷ

"Health is the true wealth of a leader; without it, no amount of success can compensate for the lack of well-being."

▷▷▷

ELEVEN

FEEDBACK AND GROWTH

Feedback is a fundamental component of personal and professional development. It serves as a mirror, reflecting our strengths and areas for improvement, and is essential for ongoing learning and adaptation. Mastering both the art of giving and receiving feedback can profoundly influence an individual's growth trajectory as well as enhance the performance of entire teams and organizations.

The Art of Giving Feedback

Giving effective feedback is a skill that requires sensitivity, clarity, and a genuine intention to help others improve. Effective feedback is constructive, specific, and actionable, aiming to guide and motivate rather than to criticize or control. It involves a delicate balance of being honest without being harsh, and supportive without being vague.

To give effective feedback, it is crucial to focus on behaviors and actions rather than on the individual's character. This approach helps prevent the recipient from feeling personally attacked and keeps the discussion centered around concrete aspects of performance that can be changed or improved.

For instance, instead of saying, "You're not good at presentations," a more constructive approach would be, "During your presentation, I noticed you read directly from the slides. It might be more engaging if you paraphrased the content and made more eye contact with the audience."

Timing and context also play significant roles in the effectiveness of feedback. Feedback should be given soon after the observed behavior to ensure that the details are fresh and relevant. Additionally, choosing an appropriate setting is important; feedback should be given in a private space where the recipient can react and respond without the pressure of public scrutiny.

Moreover, effective feedback involves a dialogue, not a monologue. This means engaging the recipient in a conversation about the feedback, allowing them to ask questions, and express their perspectives. This dialogue can lead to a deeper understanding of the feedback, foster collaboration on potential solutions, and reinforce the supportive nature of the feedback process.

The Art of Receiving Feedback

Receiving feedback graciously, whether positive or negative, is equally important. It requires openness, humility, and a commitment to self-improvement. When receiving feedback, it is vital to listen actively and resist the urge to defend or justify actions immediately.

This openness allows for a full understanding of the feedback and reflects a mature approach to personal and professional development.

One effective strategy for receiving feedback is to ask clarifying questions. This can help ensure that the feedback is fully understood and provides an opportunity to discuss practical ways to implement suggestions or make changes.

Furthermore, expressing appreciation for the feedback demonstrates recognition of the effort made by the feedback giver and can reinforce the value of a culture that supports growth and development.

Fostering Growth Through Feedback

The ultimate goal of feedback should be growth and improvement. Both giving and receiving feedback should be regular parts of the workflow in any productive environment. Organizations can foster a feedback-rich culture by training employees on effective feedback techniques and by encouraging a continuous exchange of feedback among all members.

To further enhance the impact of feedback on growth, it can be linked to specific developmental goals and followed up with support, such as training opportunities or regular check-ins to discuss progress. This follow-through shows a commitment to actual improvement and helps integrate feedback into a constructive development plan.

The Role of Feedback in Leadership

Leaders play a critical role in shaping the feedback culture of an organization. By actively giving and soliciting feedback, leaders can model the behaviors they expect to see in their teams. Leadership feedback should be exemplary in its balance of challenge and support, pushing team members to stretch and grow while providing the necessary resources and encouragement to do so.

Feedback is an invaluable tool for personal and professional development. By mastering the arts of giving and receiving feedback, individuals and organizations can create a dynamic environment where continuous improvement is the norm, and growth is actively pursued through every interaction.

Embracing feedback as a positive force can transform challenges into opportunities for learning and development, thereby fostering a culture of high performance and ongoing advancement.

ÞÞÞ

"Continual learning is the hallmark of true leadership—staying curious, embracing change, and leading the charge towards innovation and improvement."

ᐅᐅᐅ

TWELVE
NAVIGATING ETHICAL DILEMMAS

Ethical dilemmas in leadership are inevitable. As leaders ascend to higher levels of responsibility, the complexity and stakes of the decisions they must make often increase, bringing them face-to-face with challenging ethical questions. These dilemmas can involve conflicts of interest, discrepancies between organizational and personal values, or decisions that benefit one group at the expense of another. Successfully navigating these dilemmas is crucial not only for maintaining personal and organizational integrity but also for sustaining the trust and respect of colleagues, clients, and the broader community.

Understanding Ethical Dilemmas

Ethical dilemmas often arise in situations where there are competing interests or values. These are not choices between right and wrong per se, but between two rights that are in conflict. Understanding this complexity is the first step in addressing ethical dilemmas effectively. Leaders must be adept at identifying the underlying ethical principles at stake in each decision and assessing the potential impacts of different courses of action.

Developing a Framework for Ethical Decision-Making

To handle ethical dilemmas effectively, leaders can benefit from developing a consistent framework for ethical decision-making. This framework might include several steps, such as identifying all the facts, recognizing the ethical issues involved, considering who might be affected by the decision, evaluating the alternatives from multiple ethical viewpoints, and making a decision that aligns with both personal and organizational ethical standards.

One useful method is to apply established ethical tests, such as:

The Transparency Test: Would I feel comfortable if my decision were made public?

The Best Self Test: Does this decision represent who I aspire to be as a leader?

The Golden Rule Test: Would I want to be treated this way if the roles were reversed?

These tests can help leaders clarify their thinking and guide their decisions in a direction that upholds their ethical standards.

Creating an Ethical Culture

Leaders also play a pivotal role in establishing and maintaining an ethical culture within their organizations. This involves more than just dealing with dilemmas as they arise; it requires embedding ethical considerations into the fabric of the organization's daily operations. Leaders can foster an ethical culture by:

Setting a Positive Example: Demonstrate ethical behavior in all interactions. The leader's behavior sets the tone for the rest of the organization.

Communicating Expectations: Clearly articulate the organization's values and the standards of conduct expected of all employees.

Providing Training and Resources: Offer regular training on ethical issues and decision-making to ensure that all employees are equipped to handle ethical challenges.

Encouraging Open Dialogue: Create an environment where employees feel safe discussing ethical concerns and confident that such issues will be addressed seriously and respectfully.

Dealing with Ethical Breaches

When ethical breaches do occur, addressing them promptly and effectively is essential to maintain trust and accountability. This should involve a thorough investigation of the incident, followed by appropriate corrective actions, which may include disciplinary measures, changes to policies and procedures, and, if necessary, reparation to affected parties.

Leaders must handle these situations with transparency and sensitivity, acknowledging mistakes and learning from them to prevent future issues. This not only applies to breaches by team members but also to those the leader might commit. Publicly taking responsibility and outlining steps to make amends can significantly restore trust and respect.

Ethical Leadership as a Continuous Commitment

Navigating ethical dilemmas is not a one-time task but a continuous commitment. Ethical leadership requires ongoing self-reflection, education, and adaptation to new challenges and situations. Leaders must remain vigilant and proactive, regularly reviewing their decisions and behaviors to ensure they align with both evolving external standards and their personal and organizational values.

Ethical leadership is crucial for any organization aiming to sustain its credibility and integrity in the long term. By understanding ethical dilemmas, developing a solid framework for ethical decision-making, fostering an ethical culture, dealing effectively with ethical breaches, and committing to continuous ethical improvement, leaders can navigate these complex challenges successfully. This commitment not only enhances their leadership effectiveness but also builds a resilient, trustworthy, and ethical organization.

ᮠᮠᮠ

"The strength of a leader is best shown in their ability to adapt—flexibility is not a compromise but a strategic advantage."

▷▷▷

THIRTEEN

Sustainability and Social Responsibility

In the modern business landscape, sustainability and social responsibility are no longer optional but essential components of a successful and respected enterprise. These concepts go beyond environmental concerns, encompassing a broad range of practices that businesses can adopt to operate ethically, contribute positively to society, and minimize their negative impacts on the planet. For leaders, the commitment to sustainability and social responsibility is not just about risk management or compliance; it's about paving the way for a lasting legacy that benefits future generations.

Understanding Sustainability and Social Responsibility

Sustainability in business refers to practices that ensure a company's operations are environmentally sound, economically viable, and socially equitable. These practices are designed to meet the needs of the present without compromising the ability of future generations to meet their own needs. Social responsibility, on the other hand, refers to the ethical framework a company adopts to act for the benefit of society at large. This can include everything from reducing carbon footprints and enhancing labor policies to engaging in community outreach and supporting charitable causes.

The Business Case for Sustainability

Embracing sustainability can bring significant business benefits. It can lead to cost savings through more efficient use of resources and energy, which can directly improve profitability. Moreover, sustainable practices can help companies anticipate and mitigate risks associated with resource scarcity and changing regulations related to environmental protection. By planning for these changes proactively, companies can avoid costly adjustments and disruptions in the future.

In addition, sustainability often drives innovation by pushing companies to rethink products and processes that are less harmful to the environment. This can result in new product offerings and improvements that not only reduce environmental impact but also meet the changing preferences of consumers, who are increasingly favoring eco-friendly products.

Enhancing Brand Reputation and Customer Loyalty

Today's consumers, employees, and stakeholders are more environmentally conscious and expect companies to take responsibility for their ecological footprints. Companies that demonstrate genuine commitment to sustainability and social responsibility can enhance their brand reputation, which is critical in a competitive market. A strong reputation for social responsibility can attract and retain customers and employees who share the company's values, thereby fostering a loyal base.

Social Responsibility as a Driver for Employee Engagement

Engaging in socially responsible activities can also significantly enhance employee morale and engagement. Many employees prefer to work for companies that reflect their values, and they often feel more motivated and satisfied in their jobs when they see their company contributing positively to society. Furthermore, programs that encourage employee participation in community service or environmental conservation can enhance team cohesion and pride in the workplace.

Long-term Impact and Legacy

For leaders, the commitment to sustainability and social responsibility is also about legacy. By integrating these principles into the company's core strategy, leaders can ensure that their influence extends beyond immediate business results to make a positive impact on society and the environment for years to come. This legacy of responsibility can continue to guide the organization long after the original leaders have moved on, setting a standard for future generations within the company.

Implementing Effective Practices

To effectively implement sustainability and social responsibility in an organization, leaders should:

Set clear, achievable goals based on well-defined metrics for sustainability and social responsibility.

Incorporate these goals into the company's overall business strategy, ensuring they are aligned with long-term business objectives.

Engage stakeholders at all levels by communicating the importance of these practices and involving them in the decision-making process.

Report transparently on progress to build trust and accountability with stakeholders.

Navigating Challenges

Implementing sustainable and socially responsible practices is not without challenges. It requires significant upfront investment, and the benefits can take time to materialize. Leaders must navigate these challenges by fostering a culture that values long-term benefits over short-term gains and by educating stakeholders about the importance of sustainability for future competitiveness.

Sustainability and social responsibility are critical for modern businesses aiming to leave a lasting legacy. These practices not only ensure the company's operations are future-proof and ethical but also enhance its competitiveness and reputation in the long run. By embracing these principles, leaders can ensure their legacy is not only measured by financial success but also by the positive impact they have on the world.

ᗄᗄᗄ

"Mentoring is not just about building pathways for success; it's about inspiring confidence and igniting the potential within another."

▷▷▷

FOURTEEN

THE IMPACT OF COMMUNICATION

Effective communication is a pivotal skill in all aspects of life, particularly in leadership. The ability to convey information clearly, persuasively, and empathetically can significantly influence how a leader is perceived and the quality of relationships they build. This skill not only impacts interpersonal interactions but also the overall health and success of organizations. Effective communication shapes organizational culture, drives change, manages conflicts, and builds trust among teams and stakeholders.

Foundation of Effective Communication

At its core, effective communication involves the exchange of information in a way that is easily understood and appropriate to the context and audience. It encompasses not only verbal interactions but also non-verbal cues such as body language, facial expressions, and tone of voice. Effective communicators are skilled at reading these cues and adjusting their message accordingly to ensure clarity and prevent misunderstandings.

Shaping Perceptions

How leaders communicate can profoundly affect how they are perceived by others. Leaders who articulate their thoughts and intentions clearly and who regularly share insights and updates with their team are often seen as more transparent and trustworthy. Conversely, leaders who withhold information, or who communicate in an ambiguous or inconsistent manner, may be viewed as secretive or unreliable.

Effective communication also includes the ability to listen actively. Leaders who listen to their employees and respond thoughtfully are perceived as caring and respectful, which can enhance their credibility and the legitimacy of their authority. This aspect of communication not only affects how leaders are seen but also how their messages are received and followed.

Building and Maintaining Relationships

The role of communication in building and maintaining relationships is critical. Effective communication fosters strong relationships, creating networks of trust and mutual understanding. It is particularly important in managing teams, where clear and consistent communication can help align goals, clarify roles, and coordinate actions. Moreover, effective interpersonal communication—being responsive to others' concerns, offering constructive feedback, and expressing appreciation—can strengthen bonds and enhance team cohesion.

Communication also plays a crucial role in negotiation and conflict resolution. In these situations, the ability to express oneself clearly, to listen actively, and to negotiate solutions is invaluable. Effective communicators can navigate disagreements and conflicts in ways that minimize harm and preserve or even strengthen relationships.

Facilitating Organizational Effectiveness

Within organizations, communication is the glue that holds everything together. From setting strategic visions to managing everyday operations, communication skills are essential. Effective communication by leaders ensures that everyone in the organization understands the mission, values, and goals, which is crucial for aligning efforts and achieving organizational objectives.

Moreover, communication in organizations involves more than just downward transmission of information from leadership to staff. It also encompasses upward communication, where employees feel free to share their insights and feedback without fear of reprisal. This type of open communication can provide leaders with critical insights and foster a culture of innovation and continuous improvement.

Driving Change

Effective communication is also essential for driving change within organizations. Change initiatives often fail due to poor communication about the reasons for change, the benefits it will bring, and the impacts on individuals within the organization. Leaders who communicate effectively about change can help their teams understand and embrace new directions, thereby increasing the likelihood of successful implementation.

Enhancing Transparency

In the digital age, where information is more accessible than ever, transparency in communication has become increasingly important. Stakeholders, including employees, customers, and the public, expect clear and honest communication about a company's operations and challenges. Leaders who embrace this expectation and communicate openly about both successes and failures build greater trust and loyalty.

Continuous Improvement

Lastly, effective communication is not a static skill but one that requires ongoing development and adaptation. As technologies evolve and organizational contexts change, leaders must continually assess and enhance their communication strategies. This might involve adopting new communication tools, learning to communicate across diverse cultural contexts, or updating policies to reflect new communication norms.

Effective communication is a fundamental leadership skill that influences perceptions, shapes relationships, and drives organizational effectiveness. Whether through enhancing transparency, building trust, facilitating change, or resolving conflicts, the ability of leaders to communicate effectively determines their success and the health of their organizations.

ppp

"In the face of uncertainty, a leader's job is not to prevent risk but to navigate it with foresight and wisdom."

ᗡᗡᗡ

FIFTEEN

CULTIVATING COMMUNITY

Building and nurturing communities, both in personal and professional spheres, is a critical aspect of creating supportive, enriching environments where individuals can thrive. A strong community offers a network of support, shared knowledge, and mutual respect, which can enhance the lives of its members and contribute to the success of its collective goals. This guide explores strategies for cultivating such communities, emphasizing the importance of shared values, inclusive communication, and active engagement.

Establishing a Foundation of Shared Values

The cornerstone of any community is a set of shared values. These values define what the community stands for and guide its behaviors and decisions. In a professional context, this might include values such as integrity, innovation, and teamwork, while personal communities might center around shared interests or mutual support.

To identify and establish these values, it is essential to involve community members in the process. This can be achieved through workshops, surveys, and open discussions that allow members to voice what is important to them. Establishing these values collectively not only ensures that they are genuinely representative but also fosters a sense of ownership and commitment among members.

Creating Inclusive and Open Communication Channels

Effective communication is vital for the health of any community. It ensures that all members feel heard and valued, and it facilitates the effective resolution of conflicts. Creating inclusive communication channels where every member can share their thoughts and feedback is crucial. This might involve regular meetings, newsletters, online forums, or social media groups, depending on the community's size and nature.

Leaders of communities should model open communication and encourage transparency. By doing so, they set the tone for honesty and trust within the community. Training in communication skills can also be beneficial, helping members express themselves clearly and listen to others more effectively.

Fostering Engagement and Participation

Active engagement is the fuel that keeps a community vibrant and sustainable. Encouraging participation can be done through organizing regular activities that appeal to the interests and needs of the community. These activities could range from social events and volunteer projects to professional workshops and seminars.

In professional communities, creating opportunities for collaboration on projects or initiatives can further enhance engagement. When members work together towards a common goal, they develop stronger bonds and a deeper commitment to the community.

Recognizing and Utilizing Diversity

Communities are inherently diverse, comprising individuals with different backgrounds, skills, and perspectives. Recognizing and utilizing this diversity can greatly enhance the community's richness and effectiveness. Leaders should strive to understand the unique contributions of each member and find ways to incorporate them into the community's activities and decision-making processes.

Programs that highlight and celebrate diversity can also enhance community cohesion. These might include multicultural events, guest speakers from different industries, or showcases of members' hobbies and skills. Such programs not only educate but also celebrate the unique makeup of the community.

Supporting and Developing Community Members

A thriving community not only comes together but also grows together. Providing support for personal and professional development can help maintain the vitality of the community. This might involve mentorship programs, skill-building workshops, or support groups. By investing in the development of its members, a community enhances its overall strength and resilience.

Building Trust and Handling Conflicts

Trust is the glue that holds a community together. Building trust involves consistency, reliability, and fairness in all interactions within the community. Conflict is inevitable in any group dynamic, but handling it constructively is essential for maintaining trust. This can be managed through clear conflict resolution policies and regular training on how to handle disputes respectfully and effectively.

Evaluating and Evolving

Finally, communities should not be static. Regular evaluation of how the community is meeting its goals and satisfying its members' needs is crucial. This might involve periodic surveys, feedback forms, or reflection sessions. Based on these insights, the community can evolve its strategies and activities to better meet its objectives and serve its members.

Cultivating a community in any sphere requires dedication to creating a supportive environment built on shared values, inclusive communication, and active engagement. By recognizing and utilizing the diverse talents of its members and continuously evolving to meet their needs, a community can become a powerful source of support, growth, and enrichment for all involved.

"Reflecting on past experiences is not about dwelling in the past but about learning and leveraging those lessons for future successes."

❧❧❧

SIXTEEN
LEADERSHIP IN CRISIS

Effective leadership during times of crisis is crucial for navigating through turbulent periods and emerging stronger on the other side. Crises can take various forms, from economic downturns and technological failures to natural disasters and public health emergencies. Each type of crisis presents unique challenges, but the core principles of crisis leadership remain consistent: clear communication, decisive action, empathy, and resilience.

Preparation and Prevention

One of the most effective ways to manage a crisis is to prepare for it before it happens. This involves understanding potential risks and developing comprehensive crisis management plans that include clear protocols for communication, decision-making, and emergency response. Regular training sessions and drills can ensure that everyone knows their role during a crisis, reducing confusion and enabling a more effective response.

Leaders should also invest in building strong relationships with key stakeholders, including employees, customers, suppliers, and local authorities, before a crisis occurs. These relationships can provide crucial support and resources during a crisis.

Clear and Transparent Communication

During a crisis, effective communication becomes more critical than ever. Leaders must communicate regularly with their teams, stakeholders, and the public, providing clear and accurate information about the situation and the steps being taken to address it. This transparency helps to build trust and prevent the spread of rumors that can exacerbate the situation.

It's also important for leaders to communicate a sense of calm and control. While it's necessary to acknowledge the seriousness of the situation, demonstrating confidence and composure can help to stabilize the team and encourage a more focused and coordinated effort.

Decisive and Adaptive Decision-Making

Crisis situations require leaders to make decisions quickly, often with limited information. It's essential to gather as much data as possible quickly, but leaders must also be willing to make decisions based on incomplete information. Waiting too long for more information might miss opportunities to mitigate the effects of the crisis.

Moreover, as new information becomes available, leaders must be prepared to adapt their strategies. Flexibility and adaptability are key in managing a crisis effectively, as the situation can change rapidly and unexpectedly. Leaders should establish regular review points to assess the situation and adjust plans accordingly.

Empathy and Support

Leaders must also show empathy and provide support to those

affected by the crisis. This includes not only the organization's employees and their families but also customers, suppliers, and the wider community. Demonstrating genuine care and concern can help to maintain morale and motivate everyone to work together towards a common goal.

In addition to emotional support, practical support such as financial assistance, supplies, or additional resources can help those directly affected by the crisis to manage their immediate needs and start the recovery process.

Leading by Example

In times of crisis, the actions of a leader are as important as their words. Leaders who lead by example, demonstrating commitment, resilience, and a willingness to do whatever it takes to address the situation, will inspire the same qualities in their teams. This might involve taking on additional responsibilities, working longer hours, or directly engaging in frontline activities.

Post-Crisis Analysis and Learning

After the crisis has been managed, effective leaders take the time to analyze what happened, what was done to address it, and what could have been done better. This learning process is crucial for improving the organization's response to future crises. It involves detailed debriefings with key participants and stakeholders to capture lessons learned and involves updating crisis management plans to reflect these insights.

Building Resilience

Finally, crisis leadership is not just about managing the crisis itself but also about building resilience within the organization. This involves developing the ability to absorb shocks, adapt to new circumstances, and continue operating under adversity. Resilience can be built through ongoing training, flexible business models, and a strong organizational culture that values adaptability and continuous learning.

Leading effectively during times of crisis requires preparation, clear communication, decisive action, empathy, and the ability to adapt as situations change. By embodying these qualities and using these strategies, leaders can guide their organizations through crises with confidence and competence, minimizing the impact and paving the way for a successful recovery.

❧❧❧

"A leader's job is to foster an environment where diversity of thought and inclusivity are not just encouraged but celebrated."

▷▷▷

SEVENTEEN

TECHNOLOGY AND LEGACY

In the digital age, technology is not merely a tool for operational efficiency but also a powerful medium to amplify values and leave a lasting legacy. As leaders look toward the future, integrating technology strategically can extend the influence of their core values and cultural ideals far beyond the traditional confines of their organizations. This integration involves leveraging various technological platforms to communicate, model, and perpetuate values in ways that resonate across generations and geographies.

Communicating Values Through Digital Channels

The first step in leveraging technology to amplify values is through communication. Digital platforms like social media, blogs, and websites offer unprecedented opportunities to reach wide and diverse audiences. Leaders can use these platforms to share stories that exemplify their values, celebrate milestones that reflect these ideals, and comment on current events in ways that reinforce their commitment to their principles.

For instance, a company that values environmental sustainability can use its digital presence to showcase its efforts in reducing waste, supporting renewable energy projects, or developing sustainable products. This not only communicates the company's commitment to these values but also engages customers and stakeholders who share these priorities.

Modeling Values Through Corporate Practices

Technology also enables organizations to implement their values in their operational practices. From the use of environmentally friendly technologies in manufacturing to the implementation of fair and transparent AI policies that ensure ethical decision-making, technology can help embed values into the very fabric of an organization.

Additionally, technology can be used to track and measure the effectiveness of these practices. For example, data analytics can monitor the environmental impact of a company's operations over time, providing transparent reports that not only show accountability but also help in making informed decisions that align with sustainability goals.

Enhancing Accessibility and Inclusivity

One of the profound ways technology can amplify values is by enhancing accessibility and inclusivity. Technologies such as machine learning, AI, and data analytics can identify patterns of usage and barriers to access, enabling organizations to make adjustments that make their products and services more inclusive. Similarly, advancements in accessibility technology can help companies ensure that their digital content is accessible to people with disabilities, reflecting values of inclusivity and respect for diversity.

Fostering Connection and Community

Technology facilitates the building of communities by connecting people across geographical boundaries. Online platforms can host forums, webinars, and social media groups where individuals with shared values can congregate, exchange ideas, and collaborate on projects that further these values. For example, a leader passionate about education reform can create an online community that brings together educators, students, and policymakers to share resources, discuss strategies, and implement changes at various levels.

Educating and Inspiring Future Generations

Technology also plays a crucial role in education, where it can be used to inspire and teach future generations about core values. E-learning platforms, virtual reality experiences, and interactive apps can provide engaging ways to learn about critical issues like climate change, equality, and ethical business practices. By integrating values-based content into these technologies, leaders can help instill these ideals into the next generation, ensuring a lasting legacy.

Maintaining Ethical Standards in Technological Adoption

While the benefits of technology in amplifying values are significant, it is also essential to approach technological adoption ethically. This means considering the privacy implications of data collection, the socio-economic impacts of automation, and the ethical use of artificial intelligence. Leaders must ensure that the technologies they adopt and the ways they are implemented align with their core values and ethical standards.

Looking Ahead

As technology continues to evolve, it will provide even more opportunities to amplify and embed values across different spectrums of society. Leaders need to stay informed about technological trends and think creatively about how these can be aligned with their mission and values. This proactive approach ensures that their legacy is not only preserved but also enhanced in the digital age.

Technology offers a robust platform for leaders to amplify their values and build a lasting legacy. By leveraging digital communication, modeling values through corporate practices, enhancing accessibility, fostering community, and educating future generations, leaders can ensure that their core values resonate far and wide, influencing both current and future generations in meaningful ways.

ᠪᠪᠪ

"*Projecting forward isn't just about anticipating challenges; it's about actively molding the future with thoughtful intent and strategic direction.*"

ᗐᗐᗐ

EIGHTEEN

HEALTH AND WELL-BEING

The importance of physical and mental health in effective leadership cannot be overstated. Leaders who are in good health are not only able to perform their duties more effectively but also set a positive example for their teams. Maintaining optimal health allows leaders to endure the significant demands of their roles, including long hours, high stress, and the constant need for critical thinking and decision-making. This comprehensive exploration will discuss the impacts of health on leadership effectiveness and offer strategies for maintaining well-being in leadership roles.

The Impact of Physical Health on Leadership

Physical health significantly impacts a leader's energy levels, stamina, and overall performance. A leader in good physical health is better equipped to handle the rigorous demands of their role, from enduring long working hours to traveling and engaging in continuous interpersonal interactions. Good physical health also enhances cognitive function, which is crucial for decision-making and problem-solving.

Leaders with robust physical health are more likely to have a strong presence, conveying confidence and dynamism, which are essential for inspiring and motivating others. Moreover, maintaining physical health sets a powerful example for employees, promoting a culture of health within the organization.

The Role of Mental Health in Leadership

Mental health is equally critical for effective leadership. Mental well-being affects how leaders manage stress, relate to others, and make decisions. Leaders who are mentally healthy are more likely to exhibit emotional stability, resilience, and a positive attitude—all crucial qualities for effective leadership.

Good mental health allows leaders to remain calm and clear-headed in crisis situations, maintain patience, and display empathy toward team members. This capacity not only aids in better decision-making but also fosters a supportive and inclusive workplace environment.

Stress Management for Leaders

Leadership inherently involves high levels of stress due to responsibilities, expectations, and the constant need for problem-solving. Effective stress management is therefore vital for maintaining both mental and physical health. Leaders can manage stress through various techniques, such as regular physical exercise, mindfulness practices, and adequate rest.

Techniques like meditation, yoga, and deep-breathing exercises can particularly help in reducing stress and enhancing focus. Additionally, leaders should ensure they take regular breaks throughout the day to prevent burnout.

The Importance of Sleep

Sleep plays a critical role in physical and mental health. Lack of adequate sleep can impair cognitive function, mood, and overall health. Leaders must prioritize getting enough sleep to maintain their health and perform their best. Establishing a regular sleep schedule, creating a conducive sleep environment, and avoiding stimulants before bedtime can help improve sleep quality.

Nutrition and Health

Proper nutrition is foundational for good health. Leaders should focus on a balanced diet that provides all the necessary nutrients to fuel their busy days. Eating a diet rich in fruits, vegetables, lean proteins, and whole grains can boost energy levels and overall health. Moreover, staying hydrated throughout the day is crucial as dehydration can lead to decreased concentration and fatigue.

Mental Health Practices

To support mental health, leaders should engage in regular mental health practices. This might include seeking professional counseling, engaging in peer support groups, or practicing stress reduction techniques. Maintaining a healthy work-life balance is also critical. Leaders should set boundaries between their professional and personal lives, ensuring they have time to relax and enjoy activities outside of work.

Regular Health Check-Ups

Regular health check-ups are crucial for preventing health issues and managing existing conditions. Leaders should make time for annual physical exams and other necessary health screenings. Early detection of health issues can lead to better outcomes and less downtime.

Creating a Supportive Environment

Leaders also have the responsibility to create a health-supportive environment within their organizations. This can be achieved by implementing wellness programs, providing mental health resources, encouraging regular breaks, and fostering an open dialogue about health and well-being.

The health and well-being of leaders are crucial not only for their personal performance and longevity but also for the overall health of the organizations they lead. By prioritizing physical and mental health, leaders can enhance their effectiveness and set a positive example for their teams. This commitment to health can lead to a more productive, motivated, and satisfied workforce, ultimately contributing to the success and sustainability of the organization.

"Leadership involves not just guiding others to achieve goals but inspiring them to discover their own potential and pursue their passions."

ᐅᐅᐅ

NINETEEN

CONTINUAL LEARNING AND ADAPTABILITY

In an ever-evolving world, the capacity for continual learning and adaptability is not just advantageous for leaders—it is essential. The rapid pace of change in technology, market dynamics, and global economic landscapes demands that leaders remain not only current but also proactive in their learning and adaptation strategies. This ability to learn continuously and adapt effectively ensures leaders can guide their organizations through changes and challenges successfully, maintaining relevance and competitiveness.

The Necessity of Continual Learning

Continual learning is the process of constantly updating and expanding one's knowledge and skills throughout one's career. For leaders, this involves a commitment to staying informed about industry trends, technological advances, and shifts in consumer behavior. It also includes enhancing personal leadership capabilities, such as emotional intelligence, strategic thinking, and conflict resolution.

Leaders who are committed to continual learning are better prepared to handle the complexities of their roles. They are equipped to make more informed decisions, innovate more effectively, and inspire their teams through their example. Furthermore, leaders who actively pursue learning opportunities demonstrate a growth mindset—a belief that abilities can be developed through dedication and hard work. This mindset is infectious and can cultivate a culture of learning within the organization, leading to overall organizational growth and adaptability.

Adaptability in Leadership

Adaptability refers to the ability to change or adjust one's approach and strategies in response to new information, changing conditions, or unexpected obstacles. For leaders, adaptability is critical for several reasons. It allows them to pivot strategies when business models or markets evolve, respond effectively to competitive threats, and manage crises when they arise.

Adaptable leaders are also more likely to embrace innovation, as they are open to new ideas and willing to experiment. This openness can lead to breakthroughs that may significantly enhance organizational performance or disrupt conventional industry practices favorably.

Strategies for Fostering Continual Learning and Adaptability

Prioritize Education and Training: Leaders should invest in their development and encourage their teams to do the same. This could mean taking courses, attending workshops, or obtaining certifications that are relevant to their industry and roles. Many organizations also benefit from establishing in-house training programs to ensure all employees have access to continuous learning opportunities.

Leverage Technology: Modern technology offers vast resources for learning, from online courses and webinars to podcasts and virtual conferences. Leaders should utilize these tools to keep themselves and their organizations at the forefront of their fields.

Create a Learning Culture: Building a culture that values and encourages continual learning can be one of the most impactful steps a leader takes. This involves more than providing resources for learning; it requires integrating learning into the very fabric of the organization. Encouraging experimentation, celebrating educational achievements, and learning from failures are all practices that contribute to a robust learning culture.

Encourage Mentorship and Coaching: Mentorship and coaching not only facilitate personal development but also reinforce a culture of learning. Leaders can act as mentors to less experienced team members, sharing knowledge and experiences that can help guide their growth. Similarly, seeking coaches for themselves can help leaders gain new insights and stay on track with their learning goals.

Stay Curious and Open-minded: Curiosity drives learning. Leaders should cultivate an innate curiosity about how things work, how they can be improved, and what else is out there. This curiosity will naturally lead to learning and adaptation.

Practice Reflective Leadership: Reflective practice involves taking the time to consider one's actions, decisions, and their outcomes. This reflection can provide deep insights into what works well and what needs to change, guiding future learning and adaptation efforts.

The Impact of Learning and Adaptability on Organizational Success

Organizations led by continual learners are more agile, better equipped to handle change, and more innovative. These organizations can anticipate market changes more effectively and respond more rapidly to disruptions, giving them a competitive edge. Moreover, by fostering a culture of learning and adaptability, these organizations attract and retain top talent who value personal and professional growth.

Continual learning and adaptability are indispensable qualities in effective leadership. They ensure that leaders and their organizations can navigate the complexities and uncertainties of the modern business environment. By emphasizing these qualities, leaders can enhance their effectiveness, inspire their teams, and lead their organizations to sustainable success.

ᐅᐅᐅ

"*Sustainability in leadership goes beyond environmental considerations; it's about creating practices that endure and prosper over time.*"

❦❦❦

TWENTY
REFLECTING AND PROJECTING

The dual practices of reflecting and projecting are essential for effective leadership. Reflecting allows leaders to look back and evaluate past actions, decisions, and outcomes to glean insights and lessons. Projecting, on the other hand, involves looking forward to anticipate future trends, challenges, and opportunities, and planning accordingly to mitigate risks and capitalize on potential gains. Together, these practices enable leaders to cultivate wisdom from past experiences and strategically navigate toward future goals, ensuring sustained growth and relevance in a rapidly changing world.

The Importance of Self-Reflection in Leadership

Self-reflection is a critical tool for personal and professional development. It involves taking time to consider one's actions, the motivations behind them, and their impacts on others and the organization. This introspective process helps leaders identify strengths and weaknesses in their leadership style, understand the effectiveness of their interactions, and recognize areas where they can improve.

For leaders, the benefits of regular self-reflection are manifold:

Increased self-awareness: By regularly examining their thoughts and behaviors, leaders can develop a deeper understanding of who they are, what they value, and how they affect those around them.

Improved decision-making: Reflection helps leaders learn from mistakes and successes, refining their decision-making skills over time.

Enhanced emotional intelligence: Understanding one's emotional responses and learning from emotional experiences can help leaders manage their emotions more effectively, leading to better interpersonal relationships and leadership outcomes.

Alignment of personal and organizational values: Reflection helps leaders ensure that their actions and decisions are consistently aligned with their personal values and the organization's mission and vision.

Techniques for Effective Self-Reflection

Leaders can employ several techniques to make their self-reflection more structured and insightful:

Journaling: Writing down thoughts, feelings, and experiences can help leaders track their development and notice patterns over time.

Feedback solicitation: Actively seeking feedback from peers, mentors, and team members can provide external perspectives on a leader's performance, offering insights that might not be apparent through introspection alone.

Reflection rituals: Setting aside regular times for reflection, such as at the end of each day, week, or project, can help make self-reflection a consistent practice.

Coaching and mentoring: Engaging with a coach or mentor provides an opportunity for guided reflection, where leaders can discuss their experiences and gain valuable advice on how to handle similar situations in the future.

Projecting for Future Impact

While reflection focuses on the past, projecting prepares leaders for the future. Effective projecting requires a proactive approach to leadership, where future trends, potential challenges, and opportunities are continually assessed.

Strategies for Effective Projecting

Environmental scanning: Keeping abreast of technological, economic, political, and social changes that could affect the organization is crucial. This can involve regular industry analysis, attending conferences, and maintaining a network of contacts who can provide insights into emerging trends.

Scenario planning: This involves imagining possible future scenarios based on current trends and developing plans to address these potential realities. Scenario planning helps organizations prepare for unexpected changes and capitalize on possible opportunities.

Goal setting: Establishing clear, measurable, and achievable goals based on projections can guide the organization's efforts and resources towards future success.

Risk management: Identifying potential risks associated with different future scenarios and developing strategies to mitigate these risks is an essential part of projecting.

Integrating Reflection and Projection

Integrating the insights gained from reflection with the foresight developed through projection can dramatically enhance a leader's effectiveness. This integration allows leaders to learn from the past while being well-prepared for the future, ensuring that their strategies and decisions are both informed by experience and aligned with future goals.

Leaders should facilitate regular strategy reviews that incorporate both reflective insights and future projections. These reviews can help adjust plans and strategies in real-time, keeping the organization agile and aligned with both internal learnings and external changes.

Reflecting and projecting are complementary practices that, when combined, provide a robust framework for effective leadership. By regularly engaging in both, leaders can ensure that they are continuously learning from the past, prepared for the future, and capable of leading their organizations towards sustainable success. This dynamic approach to leadership not only enhances personal growth but also fosters a proactive and adaptable organizational culture.

ᐅᐅᐅ

"The art of leadership is woven from the threads of responsibility, vision, and the relentless pursuit of excellence, tied together by the consistent application of core values."

❥❥❥

TWENTY-ONE

SUMMARY

In a world where leadership is often equated with achieving high-profile successes and managing vast enterprises, this book takes a profound and introspective look at what truly makes a leader influential and memorable. This book delves into the essence of leadership that is rooted in personal values, examining how these values are not only central to effective leadership but also critical to the legacy that leaders leave behind.

The journey begins with a deep dive into the concept of legacy itself. The initial discussion centers around defining what a legacy in leadership really means and how it is shaped by more than just accomplishments or titles. It's about the enduring impact of a leader's actions and decisions, influenced strongly by their core values. The narrative emphasizes that a truly impactful legacy emerges from a consistent application of these values across all aspects of leadership, from decision-making and daily interactions to long-term strategic planning and community engagement.

The discussion transitions from the abstract to the practical by exploring how leaders can effectively embody and communicate their values. This is demonstrated through a focus on the art of communication, showing how clear, consistent, and open communication practices can not only enhance transparency but also strengthen relationships within and outside the organization. Here, the book stresses the importance of not only speaking but also listening actively, which fosters a deeper connection and understanding among team members and stakeholders.

Leadership during times of crisis receives significant attention, underscoring the pivotal role of resilience and adaptability. These sections provide a toolkit for leaders facing turbulent times, emphasizing the necessity of maintaining a calm and composed demeanor, making informed and swift decisions, and most importantly, staying true to one's core values even under pressure. The narrative illustrates how these practices not only help navigate the crisis but also reinforce a leader's reliability and commitment to their principles, which are critical components of a lasting legacy.

Further exploring the practical application of leadership values, the book discusses the integration of technology in leadership practices. It illustrates how leaders can leverage digital platforms to amplify their influence and extend the reach of their values-driven initiatives. Whether through social media, blogs, or corporate communications, technology is presented as a powerful ally in disseminating a leader's vision and values, thereby enhancing their legacy in the digital age.

The importance of personal well-being is also highlighted, with a clear message that effective leadership and personal health are inextricably linked. Leaders are encouraged to adopt healthful practices that support their physical and mental well-being, ensuring they have the stamina and clarity needed to perform their roles effectively. This section promotes not only self-care but also the creation of a workplace culture that values and supports holistic well-being, which can contribute significantly to organizational success.

As the discussion broadens to the nurturing of future leaders, mentoring and coaching are showcased as essential elements of legacy-building. By investing in the growth and development of others, leaders can pass on their values and wisdom, multiplying their impact and extending their influence far beyond their immediate presence.

Reflective practice is championed throughout as a means for continual growth and improvement. Leaders are encouraged to regularly engage in self-reflection and to foster a culture of feedback and learning within their organizations. This practice not only aids personal development but also ensures that the organization remains adaptive and responsive to change.

This book serves as a comprehensive guide for anyone aspiring to lead with integrity and impact. It offers a wealth of strategies and insights for embedding personal values into leadership practices, thereby ensuring that a leader's legacy is powerful, positive, and enduring. This book not only challenges leaders to think deeply about the kind of legacy they wish to leave but also provides them with the tools to make that vision a reality, advocating for a leadership approach that is as personally fulfilling as it is beneficial to others.

ᐅᐅᐅ

Citation And References

This book represents the culmination of extensive research and meticulous analysis, incorporating a diverse range of sources, including numerous books, scholarly studies, and personal experiences. Additionally, I have scoured various websites to gather relevant information and data essential for the compilation of this work. I have taken every precaution to ensure the accuracy of the information presented and have diligently cited all sources to acknowledge their contributions.

Despite these efforts, the possibility of inadvertent errors remains. I deeply value the insights of my readers and appreciate any feedback that can help identify and rectify such inaccuracies. I encourage you to bring any discrepancies to my attention.

Your feedback is not only welcome but crucial, as it will aid in correcting current editions and enhancing the content of future ones. I am committed to maintaining the highest standards of accuracy and reliability in my work and thank you for your support and understanding.

Additionally, I firmly uphold the principle of freedom of speech and expression as guaranteed under Article 19(1)(a) of the Constitution of India, and I respect the diverse viewpoints and expressions of all readers.

ᠹᠹᠹ

Other Books Of The Author

1. Empowering Minds: A Journey into Women's Self-Discovery and Power
2. The Dynamics of Motivation: Catalyzing Thought into Action
3. Meditation and Mental Well Being: The Path to Inner Peace and Clarity
4. The Psychology of Child Education: Nurturing Future Generations
5. Ethical Enlightenment: A Modern Guide to Living with Integrity
6. Voices of Empowerment: Stories of Women Rising Against Odds
7. Social Psychology in Everyday Life: Understanding Human Connections
8. The Essence of Motivational Speaking: Inspiring Change in Others
9. Balancing Acts: Women, Work, and the Will to Lead
10. Guiding with Grace: Raising Children with Compassion and Awareness
11. The Power of Positive Aging: Embracing Life After Fifty
12. Building Resilient Communities: Social Work in Action
13. The Ethical Educator: Principles for Teaching and Learning
14. From Insight to Impact: Social Psychology for a Better World
15. The Ethics of Empathy: A Guide to Ethical Living
16. The Science of Empowering the Self: Navigating Life's Challenges with Psychological Wisdom
17. The Mindful Conscious Leader: Meditation Techniques for Modern Management
18. Pioneering Spirit: Women's Pathways to Leadership and Empowerment
19. Feeling to Healing: The Role of Emotional Intelligence in Child Development
20. Transformative Talks and Words of Inspiration: Insights into Motivational Oratory

 PPP

Contact

Dr. Minakshi Bansal
Social Activist
Ahmedabad, Gujarat, Bharat
minakshiindiag20@yahoo.com

❧❧❧

|| LOKAHA SAMASTHAHA SUKHINO BHAVANTU ||